# Real Estate Renaissance
*Revitalizing Communities Through Investment*

NELLA BYRAN

**Copyright**

**No part of this should be reproduced without the permission of the author.**

© Nella Byran 2024

# Contents

Introduction .................................................. 4
The Vision for a Real Estate Renaissance ............. 8
Community-Centric Development ....................... 13
Mixed-Use Development: Creating Vibrant, Walkable Communities ......................................... 21
Affordable Housing Initiatives ............................ 25
Public-Private Partnerships ................................. 28
Arts and Culture Districts: Fostering Creativity and Identity in Neighborhoods .................................. 34
Sustainable Development .................................... 38
Transit-Oriented Development: Connecting Communities and Promoting Accessibility .......... 43
Small Business Support ...................................... 47
Equity and Inclusion: Ensuring Diverse Participation in the Real Estate Renaissance ....... 51
Case Studies in Community Revitalization ......... 58
Overcoming Challenges: Strategies for Addressing Obstacles in Real Estate Renaissance Projects .... 63
Conclusion ........................................................ 70

# Introduction

In the bustling tapestry of urban landscapes and the tranquil embrace of rural towns, a silent transformation is underway—a quiet revolution that promises to reshape the very fabric of our communities. Welcome to the dawn of the Real Estate Renaissance, where investment isn't just about erecting structures of steel and concrete, but about breathing life into neighborhoods, fostering inclusivity, and revitalizing the soul of our cities.

In the pages that follow, embark with us on a journey that transcends mere bricks and mortar, a journey that champions the ethos of community-centric development. This isn't just about profit margins or property values; it's about putting people first, weaving their hopes and aspirations into the very blueprint of our urban sprawls and suburban enclaves.

As we delve into the heart of this Renaissance, we'll uncover the transformative power of historic preservation and adaptive reuse. Through the lens of time-honored structures and forgotten spaces, we'll witness the alchemy of revitalization—where the echoes of the past harmonize with the pulse of the present to create something truly timeless.

Affordable housing initiatives stand as beacons of hope, addressing the fundamental right to shelter and dignity in every corner of society. But the Renaissance is not limited by nostalgia; rather, it is a celebration of innovation and diversity. Mixed-use developments emerge as lively hubs of activity, where residential, commercial, and cultural spaces converge to foster a sense of belonging and vitality.

Yet, the Renaissance is not a solitary endeavor—it thrives on collaboration. Public-private partnerships emerge as catalysts for change, bridging the gap between governmental vision and private sector expertise. Together, we'll explore the symbiotic relationship between art and urbanism, as arts and culture districts emerge as crucibles of creativity and identity, breathing new life into once-neglected neighborhoods.

But amidst the fervor of revitalization, we must not forget our stewardship of the planet. Sustainable development becomes not just a buzzword, but a guiding principle—a delicate balance between environmental responsibility and economic growth. Transit-oriented development emerges as a linchpin, knitting together disparate communities and promoting accessibility for all.

In the heart of this Renaissance lies the spirit of entrepreneurship, where small businesses stand as the lifeblood of local economies. Equity and inclusion become paramount, ensuring that the benefits of revitalization are felt by all, regardless of race, gender, or socioeconomic status.

Join us as we navigate the complex terrain of impact investing, where financial profits intertwine with social and environmental returns, paving the way for a more equitable and sustainable future. Through compelling case studies from around the globe, we'll witness the tangible impact of community revitalization, as we confront the challenges that lie ahead and chart a course for the future of community investment.

This is more than just a book—it's a manifesto for change, a call to arms for all those who believe in the transformative power of real estate to shape the world for the better. Together, let us sustain the momentum of this Renaissance and build on its success, as we strive to create communities that are not just livable, but truly thriving. Welcome to the Real Estate Renaissance—where the future begins today.

# The Vision for a Real Estate Renaissance

In the pulsating heartbeat of our cities and the serene embrace of our rural landscapes, a transformative vision is taking root—a vision that transcends the mundane transactional nature of real estate and seeks to breathe new life into our communities. Welcome to "Real Estate Renaissance: Revitalizing Communities Through Investment," where we embark on a journey of discovery, innovation, and profound impact.

In the opening chapter, aptly titled "The Vision for a Real Estate Renaissance," we set the stage for a paradigm shift in the way we perceive and engage with real estate. This isn't just about erecting buildings or maximizing profits; it's about reimagining our cities and towns as vibrant, inclusive, and sustainable spaces where people can thrive. It's about weaving a tapestry of interconnectedness, where every decision—from urban planning to development strategies—is guided by a deep-seated commitment to community well-being.

When we go into the core of this vision, we are faced with the harsh reality of our urban environments, where underprivileged people fight to find a place in a world that is constantly changing and abandoned districts linger in the shadow of progress. However, these difficulties also present an endless opportunity to promote creativity, teamwork, and transformation on a scale that goes well beyond any one city block.

Community-centric development emerges as the cornerstone of this Renaissance, where the needs and aspirations of residents take precedence over profit margins and bottom lines. We delve into the transformative power of historic preservation and adaptive reuse, where old spaces are reborn with new purpose, breathing fresh vitality into our urban cores while honoring the rich tapestry of our collective heritage.

Mixed-use development emerges as a beacon of vibrancy, where residential, commercial, and cultural spaces converge to create dynamic hubs of activity and interaction. Affordable housing initiatives stand as testaments to our commitment to social equity, ensuring that every member of society has access to safe, dignified housing, regardless of their income or background.

But the Renaissance isn't just about physical structures—it's about fostering a sense of belonging and identity within our communities. Arts and culture districts emerge as vibrant hubs of creativity, where artists, entrepreneurs, and residents come together to celebrate diversity and foster innovation. Sustainable development becomes not just a goal, but a guiding principle, as we strive to balance economic growth with environmental stewardship for the betterment of future generations.

Throughout the pages of this book, we explore the power of public-private partnerships, the importance of transit-oriented development, and the resilience of small businesses in fueling local economies. We confront the challenges that lie ahead—from bureaucratic red tape to entrenched inequality—and chart a course for overcoming them through collaboration, innovation, and unwavering determination.

Above all, though, "Real Estate Renaissance" is a monument to the revolutionary force of group effort—a call to arms for all those who think real estate can help create a more just and better future for everybody. Come along with us as we set out on this exploratory adventure and dare to imagine a world in which our towns and cities are more than just places to live; they are thriving communities where everyone has the chance to prosper and their voices are heard. Greetings from the Real Estate Renaissance, where the opportunities are as endless as our combined creativity.

# *Community-Centric Development*

In the bustling landscape of real estate development, a revolutionary ethos is taking root—one that places people at the forefront of every decision, every blueprint, and every brick laid. Welcome to "Community-Centric Development: Putting People First in Real Estate Investment," where the soul of our neighborhoods takes precedence over profit margins and where the pulse of our communities guides every step forward.

We set out on a transformative adventure in this chapter, one that redefines the fundamentals of real estate investing. Our towns and cities are now dynamic ecosystems where people's well-being, relationships, and interactions with one another are of utmost importance. They are no longer just blank canvases for massive buildings and enormous complexes. Community-centric development is a philosophy that aims to foster vibrant, inclusive communities where each person has a sense of empowerment and belonging. It is not merely a tactic.

At the heart of community-centric development lies a profound recognition of the diverse needs and aspirations of residents. It's about engaging with communities in a meaningful dialogue, listening to their concerns, and co-creating spaces that reflect their values and dreams. From neighborhood revitalization projects to large-scale urban developments, the emphasis is on fostering collaboration, transparency, and trust between developers, residents, and local stakeholders.

But community-centric development goes beyond mere consultation; it's about empowering communities to take ownership of their own destinies. Through initiatives such as community land trusts and cooperative housing models, residents are given a voice and a stake in the development process, ensuring that the benefits of investment are shared equitably among all members of society.

Moreover, community-centric development prioritizes the creation of spaces that promote social interaction, cohesion, and well-being. From vibrant public squares and green spaces to mixed-use developments that blend residential, commercial, and cultural amenities, the goal is to foster a sense of connection and belonging that transcends the boundaries of physical space.

In the pursuit of community-centric development, historic preservation and adaptive reuse emerge as powerful tools for breathing new life into old spaces. By repurposing historic buildings and landmarks, we not only honor our shared heritage but also create unique, character-rich environments that serve as focal points for community pride and identity.

Affordable housing initiatives stand as pillars of social equity within the realm of community-centric development, ensuring that housing remains accessible and affordable for residents of all income levels. Through innovative financing mechanisms and inclusive zoning policies, we strive to create diverse, inclusive communities where individuals from all walks of life can thrive and prosper.

Developing a culture of understanding, kindness, and unity in our communities is possibly the most crucial aspect of community-centric growth. It all comes down to realizing that a community's pleasure and well-being, rather than its GDP or skyline, are the genuine indicators of its success. Let's keep in mind that the real value of real estate investment is not in the buildings we develop, but rather in the communities we support and the lives we touch as we set out on this transformative journey. Greetings from the era of community-centered development, where the needs of people always come first.

# Historic Preservation and Adaptive Reuse

In the tapestry of our cities, woven through the threads of time, lie forgotten gems—historic buildings that whisper tales of bygone eras, their walls echoing with the footfalls of generations past. Yet, amidst the march of progress, these architectural treasures often find themselves at risk of fading into obscurity. Enter "Historic Preservation and Adaptive Reuse: Breathing New Life into Old Spaces," where the art of honoring the past meets the innovation of the present, ushering in a renaissance of revitalization and renewal.

We set out on a voyage of rediscovery in this chapter, one that honors the enduring beauty and inherent worth of our constructed heritage. Historic preservation is more than just a sentimental gesture; it is a physical link to our common history, a declaration of our shared identity, and a reminder of the rich tapestry of human experience that has developed over time.

At the heart of historic preservation lies a profound reverence for craftsmanship, artistry, and ingenuity. From grandiose landmarks to humble vernacular structures, each historic building tells a story—a story of triumph and tragedy, of innovation and perseverance, of the countless lives that have passed through its doors. By preserving these buildings, we not only honor the past but also create opportunities for future generations to connect with their cultural roots and heritage.

But historic preservation is more than just a preservationist's endeavor; it is a catalyst for economic revitalization and community development. Through adaptive reuse—the practice of repurposing historic buildings for contemporary uses—we breathe new life into old spaces, transforming dilapidated structures into vibrant hubs of activity, creativity, and commerce.

From repurposing old warehouses into trendy loft apartments to transforming former factories into bustling mixed-use developments, adaptive reuse unlocks the hidden potential of historic buildings, infusing them with new purpose while preserving their intrinsic character and charm. In doing so, we not only breathe new life into old spaces but also create unique, character-rich environments that serve as focal points for community pride and identity.

Moreover, historic preservation and adaptive reuse offer tangible environmental benefits, helping to mitigate the carbon footprint associated with new construction while conserving valuable resources and embodied energy. By repurposing existing buildings, we reduce the need for demolition and construction, thereby minimizing waste and preserving the embodied history and craftsmanship embedded within their walls.

Yet, the path to historic preservation and adaptive reuse is not without its challenges. From regulatory hurdles to financial constraints, developers and preservationists alike must navigate a complex landscape of competing interests and priorities. However, the rewards far outweigh the challenges, as historic preservation not only enhances property values and stimulates economic growth but also fosters a sense of place, identity, and belonging within our communities.

As we embark on this journey of rediscovery and renewal, let us embrace the transformative power of historic preservation and adaptive reuse, cherishing the past while building towards a brighter, more sustainable future. Together, let us breathe new life into old spaces, preserving the stories of our past for generations yet to come. Welcome to the world of Historic Preservation and

Adaptive Reuse—where the echoes of history resonate with the promise of tomorrow.

## *Mixed-Use Development: Creating Vibrant, Walkable Communities*

In the bustling landscape of urban development, a paradigm shift is underway—a shift that redefines the way we conceive of and interact with our built environment. Welcome to "Mixed-Use Development: Creating Vibrant, Walkable Communities," where the boundaries between live, work, and play blur, giving rise to dynamic, interconnected spaces that pulse with life and energy.

At the heart of mixed-use development lies a simple yet profound idea: integration. No longer are our cities and neighborhoods mere collections of isolated buildings; they are vibrant ecosystems where residential, commercial, and cultural activities coexist in harmony. Mixed-use development isn't just about constructing buildings; it's about creating communities—places where people can live, work, shop, dine, and socialize—all within easy reach of one another.

In this chapter, we explore the transformative power of mixed-use development in fostering vibrant, walkable communities. Gone are the days of sprawling suburbs and monotonous office parks; in their place emerge lively, pedestrian-friendly neighborhoods where every street corner holds the promise of discovery and connection.

One of the defining features of mixed-use development is its emphasis on walkability. By clustering a variety of amenities within close proximity, mixed-use developments encourage residents to ditch the car in favor of more sustainable modes of transportation. From cozy cafes and boutique shops to bustling markets and green spaces, everything is just a short stroll away, fostering a sense of community and reducing reliance on automobiles.

But mixed-use development isn't just about convenience—it's about creating spaces that are vibrant and diverse, where people of all ages and backgrounds can come together to live, work, and play. By integrating residential units with commercial and cultural spaces, mixed-use developments foster a sense of social interaction and cohesion, enriching the fabric of community life.

Moreover, mixed-use development offers tangible economic benefits, stimulating local economies and enhancing property values. By creating a diverse mix of uses, developers can attract a broad range of tenants and customers, ensuring that their investments remain resilient in the face of economic fluctuations. Meanwhile, residents enjoy the convenience of having essential services and amenities right at their doorstep, enhancing their quality of life and sense of well-being.

But perhaps most importantly, mixed-use development is about fostering a sense of place—a sense of belonging and identity within our neighborhoods. By creating vibrant, walkable communities where people can live, work, and play, we not only enhance the physical environment but also cultivate a sense of pride and attachment among residents.

As we embrace the principles of mixed-use development, let us reimagine our cities and neighborhoods as vibrant, interconnected spaces where the lines between public and private, residential and commercial, blur into a seamless tapestry of urban life. Together, let us create communities that are not just places to live, but vibrant, thriving ecosystems where every individual has the opportunity to flourish. Welcome to the world of Mixed-Use

Development—where the streets are alive with possibility, and every corner holds the promise of connection and discovery.

## *Affordable Housing Initiatives*

In the ever-evolving narrative of urban development, one pressing issue stands at the forefront: the urgent need for affordable housing. Welcome to "Affordable Housing Initiatives: Addressing the Housing Needs of Every Community," where we confront the stark reality of housing insecurity head-on and chart a course towards a more equitable and inclusive future.

In this chapter, we embark on a journey of empathy, innovation, and collective action—a journey that seeks to ensure that every member of society has access to safe, dignified housing, regardless of their income or background. Affordable housing isn't just a social issue; it's a fundamental human right, a cornerstone of vibrant, healthy communities, and a prerequisite for individual and collective well-being.

At the heart of affordable housing initiatives lies a deep-seated commitment to social equity and economic justice. From government-led programs to private sector innovations, a variety of approaches are being deployed to address the complex web of factors that contribute to housing affordability—from land use policies and zoning regulations to construction costs and financing mechanisms.

One of the key strategies in the fight for affordable housing is the development of subsidized housing units specifically targeted towards low and moderate-income households. Through a combination of public subsidies, tax incentives, and regulatory mechanisms, developers are able to create housing that is affordable to those who need it most, ensuring that no one is left behind in the quest for safe and stable housing.

But affordable housing initiatives go beyond simply building new units; they also encompass a wide range of interventions aimed at preserving existing affordable housing stock and preventing displacement. From rent stabilization programs and tenant protections to community land trusts and cooperative housing models, these initiatives seek to ensure that vulnerable communities are not displaced by gentrification and rising housing costs.

Moreover, affordable housing initiatives recognize the interconnectedness of housing with other social determinants of health and well-being. By ensuring access to affordable housing, we not only address homelessness and housing insecurity but also improve educational outcomes, reduce healthcare costs, and promote economic stability and upward mobility for individuals and families.

But perhaps most importantly, affordable housing initiatives are about fostering a sense of belonging and community within our neighborhoods. By creating diverse, inclusive communities where people of all income levels can live side by side, we not only enhance social cohesion but also challenge stereotypes and break down barriers of segregation and inequality.

As we navigate the complex terrain of affordable housing, let us remember that the true measure of our success lies not in the number of units built or dollars invested, but in the impact we have on the lives of individuals and families. Together, let us forge a future where housing is not a privilege but a right, where every member of society has access to safe, dignified housing, and where communities are defined not by wealth or status, but by compassion, solidarity, and inclusion. Welcome to the world of Affordable Housing Initiatives—where every door opens onto the promise of a brighter tomorrow.

# *Public-Private Partnerships*

In the intricate dance of urban renewal and community revitalization, one key player stands out: the collaboration between the public and private sectors. Welcome to "Public-Private Partnerships: Collaboration for Community Revitalization," where we explore the transformative power of bringing together government agencies, private developers, and community stakeholders to breathe new life into our neighborhoods and urban centers.

In this chapter, we delve into the dynamics of public-private partnerships (PPPs) as a catalyst for positive change—a marriage of vision, resources, and expertise that transcends traditional boundaries and fosters innovation, efficiency, and inclusivity in the realm of community development.

At the heart of public-private partnerships lies a shared commitment to the common good—a recognition that the challenges facing our communities are too complex and multifaceted to be tackled by any single entity alone. By pooling together their respective strengths and resources, public and private partners are able to leverage their collective expertise and capacity to deliver projects that are greater than the sum of their parts.

One of the key advantages of public-private partnerships is their ability to unlock new sources of funding and financing for community revitalization projects. By tapping into private capital markets and leveraging public resources, PPPs are able to bridge funding gaps and overcome financial barriers that might otherwise impede progress. From infrastructure improvements to affordable housing developments, PPPs offer a flexible and scalable model for financing projects of all sizes and scopes.

But public-private partnerships are about more than just money—they're about collaboration, innovation, and shared accountability. By bringing together a diverse array of stakeholders—including government agencies, local businesses, community organizations, and residents—PPPs ensure that projects are informed by the needs and priorities of the communities they serve. Through transparent decision-making processes and meaningful community engagement, PPPs empower residents to play an active role in shaping the future of their neighborhoods and cities.

Moreover, public-private partnerships offer a framework for delivering projects with greater efficiency and effectiveness. By harnessing the strengths of both the public and private sectors, PPPs are able to streamline project delivery processes, minimize bureaucratic red tape, and maximize the impact of limited resources. From streamlined permitting and regulatory approvals to innovative design-build procurement methods, PPPs offer a nimble and responsive approach to community revitalization that is often lacking in traditional government-led initiatives.

But perhaps most importantly, public-private partnerships are about creating lasting, sustainable change in our communities. By aligning the interests of public and private partners around shared goals and objectives, PPPs ensure that projects are designed with the long-term well-being of communities in mind. Whether it's revitalizing blighted neighborhoods, spurring economic development, or addressing pressing social and environmental challenges, PPPs offer a collaborative and holistic approach to community revitalization that holds the promise of a brighter future for all.

As we navigate the complex terrain of urban development and community revitalization, let us embrace the transformative potential of public-private partnerships as a catalyst for positive change. Together, let us forge a future where collaboration, innovation, and inclusivity are the hallmarks of community development, and where the power of partnership is harnessed to create vibrant, resilient, and equitable communities for generations to come. Welcome to the world of Public-Private Partnerships—where collaboration knows no bounds, and the possibilities are endless.

# Arts and Culture Districts: Fostering Creativity and Identity in Neighborhoods

Step into the vibrant tapestry of urban life, where the pulse of creativity beats in every corner and the spirit of identity dances in the streets. Welcome to "Arts and Culture Districts: Fostering Creativity and Identity in Neighborhoods," where we celebrate the transformative power of artistic expression and cultural heritage in shaping the soul of our communities.

In this chapter, we embark on a journey of exploration—a journey that celebrates the rich diversity of human creativity and the profound impact it has on the fabric of our neighborhoods. Arts and culture districts aren't just spaces for passive consumption; they are dynamic hubs of activity, innovation, and collaboration, where artists, entrepreneurs, and residents come together to breathe life into our urban landscapes.

At the heart of arts and culture districts lies a profound recognition of the intrinsic value of artistic expression and cultural heritage. From street murals and public sculptures to performance spaces and community festivals, these districts serve as living canvases that reflect the stories, traditions, and aspirations of the communities they inhabit. By celebrating the unique cultural identities of our neighborhoods, arts and culture districts foster a sense of pride, belonging, and connection among residents, strengthening the social fabric and enhancing the quality of life for all.

But arts and culture districts are more than just aesthetic enhancements; they are powerful engines of economic development and community revitalization. By attracting tourists, visitors, and patrons from near and far, these districts generate economic activity, support local businesses, and create jobs, revitalizing blighted neighborhoods and breathing new life into struggling commercial corridors. Moreover, arts and culture districts serve as catalysts for urban regeneration, spurring investment, and redevelopment in areas that were once overlooked or neglected.

Moreover, arts and culture districts serve as platforms for social and environmental change, fostering dialogue, understanding, and empathy across diverse communities. By providing spaces for dialogue, reflection, and engagement, these districts promote social cohesion, bridge cultural divides, and empower individuals and communities to address pressing social and environmental challenges. Whether it's through public art installations that spark conversations about social justice or community workshops that explore sustainable living practices, arts and culture districts offer myriad opportunities for creative expression and collective action.

But perhaps most importantly, arts and culture districts are about fostering a sense of joy, wonder, and possibility within our communities. By infusing our neighborhoods with beauty, creativity, and imagination, these districts inspire us to see the world with fresh eyes, to embrace the unfamiliar, and to celebrate the richness and diversity of human experience. As we navigate the complexities of urban life, let us remember the transformative power of the arts to heal, to inspire, and to unite us in our common humanity. Welcome to the world of Arts and Culture Districts—where creativity knows no bounds, and every street corner holds the promise of discovery and delight.

# Sustainable Development

In the intricate dance of progress and preservation, there exists a delicate balance—a balance between the imperatives of economic growth and the imperative of environmental responsibility. Welcome to "Sustainable Development: Balancing Environmental Responsibility with Economic Growth," where we embark on a journey of innovation, stewardship, and collective action to chart a course towards a more sustainable future for all.

At the heart of sustainable development lies a profound recognition of the interconnectedness of our social, economic, and environmental systems. It is a holistic approach that seeks to meet the needs of the present without compromising the ability of future generations to meet their own needs. From renewable energy and green infrastructure to circular economies and regenerative agriculture, sustainable development offers a roadmap for reconciling human progress with planetary health.

In this chapter, we delve into the principles and practices of sustainable development, exploring how we can harness the power of innovation and collaboration to build a more resilient and equitable world. Sustainable development isn't just about mitigating environmental impact; it's about creating thriving, inclusive communities where every individual has the opportunity to flourish, regardless of their background or circumstances.

One of the key pillars of sustainable development is environmental stewardship—a commitment to protecting and preserving our natural resources for future generations. From reducing greenhouse gas emissions and mitigating climate change to conserving biodiversity and safeguarding ecosystems, sustainable development seeks to ensure that our planet remains habitable and hospitable for all forms of life.

But sustainable development is also about economic prosperity—a recognition that environmental responsibility and economic growth are not mutually exclusive, but rather mutually reinforcing. By investing in clean energy, sustainable infrastructure, and green technologies, we can create jobs, stimulate innovation, and drive economic growth while simultaneously reducing our environmental footprint and enhancing the resilience of our communities.

Moreover, sustainable development is about social equity—a commitment to ensuring that the benefits of progress are shared equitably among all members of society. From affordable housing and access to healthcare to education and economic opportunity, sustainable development seeks to address the root causes of poverty and inequality, empowering individuals and communities to reach their full potential.

But perhaps most importantly, sustainable development is about collective action—a recognition that the challenges we face are too complex and interconnected to be addressed by any single entity alone. It is about coming together as governments, businesses, communities, and individuals to forge a common path forward—a path that honors the diversity of human experience and the interconnectedness of all life on Earth.

As we navigate the uncertain waters of the 21st century, let us embrace the principles of sustainable development as a guiding light—a beacon of hope and possibility in a world of uncertainty and upheaval. Together, let us build a future where economic prosperity is inextricably linked to environmental stewardship and social equity, and where every individual has the opportunity to thrive in harmony with the planet.

Welcome to the world of Sustainable Development—where the possibilities are as vast as our collective imagination, and the promise of a better tomorrow shines bright.

# Transit-Oriented Development: Connecting Communities and Promoting Accessibility

Step aboard the train of progress and embark on a journey towards a more connected, accessible future. Welcome to "Transit-Oriented Development: Connecting Communities and Promoting Accessibility," where we explore the transformative power of integrated transportation systems in shaping the fabric of our cities and neighborhoods.

In this chapter, we embark on a voyage of exploration—a voyage that celebrates the convergence of mobility and urban development, and the profound impact it has on the accessibility, livability, and sustainability of our communities. Transit-oriented development (TOD) isn't just about building transit infrastructure; it's about creating vibrant, walkable neighborhoods where people can live, work, and play—all within easy reach of efficient and reliable public transportation.

At the heart of transit-oriented development lies a simple yet powerful idea: accessibility. By locating housing, employment, and amenities within close proximity to transit hubs, TOD seeks to reduce reliance on private automobiles, alleviate traffic congestion, and promote more sustainable modes of transportation. From bustling transit plazas to pedestrian-friendly streetscapes, TOD fosters a sense of connectivity and mobility that transcends traditional barriers of distance and geography.

In this chapter, we'll explore the key principles and practices of transit-oriented development, from transit-oriented design and land use planning to community engagement and economic development. By integrating transit infrastructure with mixed-use development, green space, and active transportation options, TOD creates vibrant, inclusive neighborhoods that are accessible to people of all ages, incomes, and abilities.

But transit-oriented development is more than just a planning strategy; it's a catalyst for positive change—a driver of economic growth, social equity, and environmental sustainability. By fostering compact, walkable neighborhoods served by high-quality transit, TOD attracts investment, stimulates economic activity, and creates jobs, revitalizing urban cores and suburban centers alike. Moreover, by providing affordable, convenient transportation options, TOD expands access to opportunity, reducing transportation costs and improving quality of life for residents across the socioeconomic spectrum.

But perhaps most importantly, transit-oriented development is about fostering a sense of community—a recognition that the places we inhabit are not just collections of buildings, but interconnected networks of people, places, and experiences. By creating vibrant, transit-oriented neighborhoods where people can live, work, and play in close proximity to one another, TOD strengthens social connections, fosters a sense of belonging, and promotes a culture of sustainability and shared responsibility.

As we navigate the complexities of urban development and transportation planning, let us embrace the principles of transit-oriented development as a blueprint for building more connected, accessible, and inclusive communities. Together, let us embark on a journey towards a future where mobility is not just a means of getting from point A to point B, but a catalyst for building stronger, more resilient, and more vibrant communities for generations to come. Welcome to the world of Transit-Oriented Development—where the journey is just as important as the destination, and every stop holds the promise of possibility and connection.

# Small Business Support

Step into the vibrant marketplace of local economies, where the heartbeat of community thrives in the entrepreneurial spirit of small businesses. Welcome to "Small Business Support: Fueling Local Economies through Real Estate Investment," where we explore the pivotal role of real estate in nurturing the growth, resilience, and prosperity of small businesses.

In this chapter, we embark on a journey of discovery—a journey that celebrates the symbiotic relationship between small businesses and the built environment, and the transformative impact it has on the economic vitality and social fabric of our neighborhoods.

At the heart of small business support lies a simple yet profound idea: localism. By investing in small businesses and fostering a culture of entrepreneurship, we not only create jobs and stimulate economic activity but also cultivate a sense of community pride, identity, and belonging. From family-owned shops and neighborhood cafes to artisanal boutiques and creative co-working spaces, small businesses are the lifeblood of our local economies, enriching our neighborhoods with diversity, character, and vitality.

In this chapter, we'll explore the myriad ways in which real estate investment can support and empower small businesses, from providing affordable commercial space to fostering vibrant mixed-use developments that serve as incubators for innovation and creativity. By offering flexible leasing terms, access to capital, and supportive infrastructure, real estate developers and investors can create the conditions for small businesses to thrive, grow, and succeed.

But small business support is about more than just economics; it's about community building. By creating spaces where people can gather, connect, and collaborate, small businesses serve as anchors of social cohesion, bridging divides and fostering a sense of belonging among residents. Moreover, by sourcing goods and services locally, small businesses help to circulate wealth within the community, strengthening the local economy and reducing reliance on external markets.

But perhaps most importantly, small business support is about empowerment—a recognition that entrepreneurship is not just a means of making a living, but a pathway to self-determination, dignity, and fulfillment. By providing opportunities for individuals to pursue their passions, build wealth, and create a legacy for future generations, small businesses empower individuals and families to chart their own course towards prosperity and success.

As we navigate the complexities of urban development and economic revitalization, let us embrace the power of small business support as a catalyst for positive change. Together, let us invest in the dreams and aspirations of local entrepreneurs, building stronger, more resilient, and more inclusive communities where every individual has the opportunity to thrive. Welcome to the world of Small Business Support—where the spirit of enterprise knows no bounds, and the possibilities for growth and prosperity are limitless.

# Equity and Inclusion: Ensuring Diverse Participation in the Real Estate Renaissance

Step into the realm of real estate renaissance, where every brick laid and every decision made is infused with the spirit of equity and inclusion. Welcome to "Equity and Inclusion: Ensuring Diverse Participation in the Real Estate Renaissance," where we explore the imperative of embracing diversity and fostering inclusive practices in every facet of community development.

In this chapter, we embark on a journey of introspection—a journey that challenges us to confront the systemic barriers and inequalities that have long plagued the real estate industry and to chart a course towards a more just, equitable, and inclusive future.

At the heart of equity and inclusion lies a simple yet profound principle: everyone deserves a seat at the table. From developers and investors to residents and stakeholders, the real estate renaissance must be a collective endeavor—one that reflects the rich diversity of our communities and ensures that the benefits of progress are shared equitably among all.

In this chapter, we'll explore the ways in which equity and inclusion can be woven into the fabric of real estate development, from promoting diversity in hiring and contracting to prioritizing the needs and aspirations of marginalized communities in planning and decision-making processes. By centering the voices and experiences of those who have been historically marginalized and excluded, we can create spaces that are truly reflective of the values and aspirations of our diverse society.

But equity and inclusion are not just moral imperatives; they are also economic imperatives. By embracing diversity and fostering inclusive practices, real estate developers and investors can tap into new markets, unlock untapped talent, and drive innovation and creativity. Moreover, by prioritizing the needs of underserved communities, we can create opportunities for economic empowerment and wealth creation, lifting up those who have been left behind by traditional development paradigms.

But perhaps most importantly, equity and inclusion are about justice—a recognition that the legacy of past injustices continues to shape the present and that we have a moral obligation to address the structural inequalities that perpetuate disparities in access to housing, opportunity, and wealth. By dismantling barriers to participation and investing in equitable development strategies, we can create a future where everyone has the opportunity to thrive, regardless of race, gender, ethnicity, or socioeconomic status.

As we navigate the complexities of urban development and community revitalization, let us embrace the principles of equity and inclusion as guiding lights, illuminating the path towards a more just, equitable, and inclusive future for all. Together, let us build a real estate renaissance that reflects the richness and diversity of our communities and ensures that no one is left behind in the march towards progress. Welcome to the world of Equity and Inclusion—where diversity is celebrated, and everyone has a stake in shaping the future.

Impact Investing: Generating Social and Environmental Returns Alongside Financial Profits

Step into the realm of investing with purpose, where financial gains intertwine with social and environmental impact. Welcome to "Impact Investing: Generating Social and Environmental

Returns alongside Financial Profits," where we explore the transformative power of aligning capital with conscience to drive positive change in our communities and the world.

In this chapter, we embark on a journey of discovery—a journey that challenges traditional notions of investment and wealth accumulation and invites us to redefine success in terms of not just financial returns, but also social and environmental outcomes.

At the heart of impact investing lies a simple yet profound idea: that capital has the power to be a force for good. From affordable housing and renewable energy to community development and social enterprise, impact investing seeks to deploy capital in ways that generate positive social and environmental returns alongside financial profits.

In this chapter, we'll explore the principles and practices of impact investing, from identifying investment opportunities that align with our values and priorities to measuring and managing the social and environmental impact of our investments. By leveraging a wide range of financial instruments, including venture capital, private equity, and debt financing, impact investors can support innovative solutions to some of the world's most pressing challenges, from poverty and inequality to climate change and environmental degradation.

But impact investing is about more than just doing good—it's also about doing well. By targeting investments that generate both social and financial returns, impact investors can achieve competitive financial performance while also making a positive difference in the world. Moreover, by aligning their investments with their values and priorities, impact investors can derive a deeper sense of fulfillment and purpose from their financial endeavors, knowing that their capital is being used to create positive change.

But perhaps most importantly, impact investing is about empowerment—a recognition that we all have the power to shape the future through our investment choices. By channeling our capital towards businesses and projects that reflect our values and priorities, we can help to build a more just, equitable, and sustainable world for future generations.

As we navigate the complexities of the global economy and the challenges facing our communities and the planet, let us embrace the principles of impact investing as a guiding light, illuminating the path towards a more prosperous, inclusive, and sustainable future for all. Together, let us harness the power of capital to drive positive change in the world and create a legacy that extends far beyond financial returns. Welcome to the world of Impact Investing—where profits and purpose converge, and every investment is an opportunity to make a difference.

# *Case Studies in Community Revitalization*

Welcome to the heart of community revitalization—a collection of inspiring tales, showcasing the resilience, innovation, and spirit of collaboration that breathe new life into neighborhoods around the globe. In this chapter, "Case Studies in Community Revitalization: Success Stories from Around the Globe," we embark on a journey of discovery, exploring real-world examples of transformative change that have turned blight into beauty, despair into hope, and fragmentation into unity.

Each case study is a testament to the power of vision, leadership, and collective action in revitalizing communities and creating a brighter future for all. From bustling urban centers to rural hamlets, these success stories illustrate the diverse approaches and strategies that can be deployed to address the unique challenges and opportunities facing communities around the world.

In Detroit, Michigan, once the poster child for urban decline, we find a story of resilience and reinvention. Through innovative partnerships between government, philanthropy, and the private sector, abandoned buildings have been transformed into vibrant mixed-use developments, blighted neighborhoods have been revitalized, and a sense of optimism and pride has been restored to the Motor City.

In Medellín, Colombia, once synonymous with violence and despair, we find a story of transformation and renewal. Through visionary leadership and bold investments in public infrastructure and social programs, the city has been transformed into a model of urban innovation and inclusivity. From the iconic Metrocable system that connects hillside slums to the city center to the vibrant public spaces and cultural amenities that have sprung up in once-neglected neighborhoods, Medellín offers a powerful example of how investment in social infrastructure can transform lives and communities.

In Kigali, Rwanda, a city scarred by genocide and conflict, we find a story of reconciliation and renewal. Through deliberate efforts to foster social cohesion and economic opportunity, Kigali has emerged as a beacon of hope and resilience in the heart of Africa. From the bustling markets and vibrant street life of the city center to the lush green spaces and modern amenities that dot the landscape, Kigali offers a powerful example of how investment in community development can catalyze positive change and build a brighter future for all.

And in Copenhagen, Denmark, a city renowned for its commitment to sustainability and livability, we find a story of innovation and inspiration. Through investments in green infrastructure, sustainable transportation, and participatory planning processes, Copenhagen has become a global leader in urban sustainability and quality of life. From the iconic bike lanes and pedestrian-friendly streets that crisscross the city to the vibrant public spaces and cultural amenities that define its urban landscape, Copenhagen offers a powerful example of how cities can prioritize people and the planet while still fostering economic growth and prosperity.

These are just a few of the countless success stories in community revitalization happening around the globe. Each case study offers valuable lessons and insights into the principles and practices that underpin successful community development efforts, from the importance of inclusive decision-making and community engagement to the power of strategic investments in infrastructure and social programs. As we continue on our journey of discovery, let us draw inspiration from these stories and redouble our efforts to create vibrant, resilient, and inclusive communities where everyone has the opportunity to thrive. Welcome to the world of community revitalization—where every success story is a testament to the power of vision, collaboration, and hope.

## *Overcoming Challenges: Strategies for Addressing Obstacles in Real Estate Renaissance Projects*

In the landscape of real estate renaissance, challenges abound—yet within every obstacle lies an opportunity for innovation, resilience, and growth. Welcome to "Overcoming Challenges: Strategies for Addressing Obstacles in Real Estate Renaissance Projects," where we embark on a journey of exploration, uncovering the tools, tactics, and tenacity needed to navigate the complexities of community development and urban renewal.

In this chapter, we confront head-on the myriad challenges that can impede progress in real estate renaissance projects—from regulatory hurdles and financial constraints to community opposition and market volatility. But far from being insurmountable barriers, these challenges are catalysts for creative problem-solving and collaborative action.

At the heart of overcoming challenges lies a spirit of resilience—a willingness to adapt, innovate, and persevere in the face of adversity. Whether it's navigating the complexities of zoning and permitting processes or securing financing in a tight credit market, successful real estate developers and investors approach challenges with a sense of determination and resourcefulness, seeking out creative solutions and forging strategic partnerships to achieve their goals.

In this chapter, we'll explore a range of strategies for addressing common obstacles in real estate renaissance projects, drawing on real-world examples and best practices from around the globe. From leveraging public-private partnerships and community engagement to mitigating risk and building resilience through diversification, there are myriad approaches that developers and investors can take to overcome challenges and unlock the full potential of their projects.

But perhaps the most important strategy for overcoming challenges in real estate renaissance projects is collaboration. By bringing together diverse stakeholders—including government agencies, community organizations, financial institutions, and residents—developers and investors can tap into a wealth of knowledge, expertise, and resources that can help to overcome even the most daunting obstacles.

Moreover, by engaging with local communities and incorporating their input and feedback into the planning and development process, developers and investors can build trust, foster buy-in, and create projects that are truly reflective of the needs and aspirations of the people they serve.

As we navigate the complexities of real estate development and community revitalization, let us embrace the challenges that lie ahead as opportunities for growth and transformation. Together, let us draw on our collective ingenuity, resilience, and determination to overcome obstacles and build a future where every neighborhood is vibrant, inclusive, and resilient. Welcome to the world of overcoming challenges—where every obstacle is an opportunity, and every setback is a stepping stone towards success.

# *The Future of Community Investment: Sustaining Momentum and Building on Success*

As we stand at the threshold of a new era in community investment, the future beckons with promise and possibility. Welcome to "The Future of Community Investment: Sustaining Momentum and Building on Success," where we embark on a journey of anticipation and aspiration, charting a course towards a more vibrant, resilient, and inclusive future for all.

In this final chapter, we look ahead to the challenges and opportunities that lie on the horizon, and explore the strategies and principles that will guide us as we seek to sustain momentum and build on the successes of the past.

At the heart of the future of community investment lies a commitment to sustainability—a recognition that the decisions we make today will shape the world of tomorrow. From embracing green infrastructure and renewable energy to promoting equitable development and social inclusion, sustainable community investment offers a roadmap for creating thriving, resilient communities that can withstand the challenges of the 21st century.

In this chapter, we'll explore the key trends and drivers shaping the future of community investment, from the rise of impact investing and social entrepreneurship to the growing emphasis on resilience and adaptive capacity in the face of climate change and other global challenges. By embracing innovation and harnessing the power of technology, data, and collaboration, we can unlock new opportunities for positive change and create lasting impact in communities around the world.

But the future of community investment is not just about technology and innovation; it's also about people and partnerships. By fostering collaboration and building bridges across sectors and silos, we can create more inclusive and equitable communities where everyone has the opportunity to thrive. From public-private partnerships and community-driven initiatives to cross-sectoral collaborations and collective impact efforts, the future of community investment is grounded in the principle of shared ownership and shared responsibility for the well-being of our communities.

Moreover, the future of community investment is about resilience—a recognition that the challenges facing our communities are complex, interconnected, and ever-evolving. By investing in infrastructure, education, and social capital, we can build communities that are better prepared to weather the storms of the future and bounce back stronger and more resilient than ever before.

As we look to the future of community investment, let us embrace the possibilities that lie ahead with hope and optimism. Together, let us continue to work tirelessly to build a future where every community is vibrant, inclusive, and sustainable—a future where everyone has the opportunity to thrive and reach their full potential. Welcome to the world of the future of community investment—where the possibilities are endless, and the journey is just beginning.

# Conclusion

In conclusion, "Real Estate Renaissance: Revitalizing Communities Through Investment" has been a journey of exploration, inspiration, and empowerment—a testament to the transformative power of collective action and visionary leadership in shaping the future of our communities. Throughout these pages, we have delved into the principles and practices of community investment, from affordable housing initiatives and transit-oriented development to impact investing and small business support. We have explored the challenges and opportunities facing real estate renaissance projects, and we have celebrated the successes and innovations that are driving positive change in neighborhoods around the globe.

But our journey does not end here. As we look to the future, we are reminded that the work of community investment is never finished. There are still challenges to overcome, inequalities to address, and opportunities to seize. Yet, as we stand on the cusp of a new era in community development, we do so with hope and optimism, knowing that the seeds of change have been planted and that the momentum for progress is building.

Let us continue to build on the successes of the past, to innovate and adapt to the challenges of the present, and to work tirelessly towards a future where every community is vibrant, resilient, and inclusive. Together, let us harness the power of real estate investment to create a world where everyone has access to safe, affordable housing, where small businesses thrive, and where transit connects us in more ways than one.

As we close the final chapter of this book, let us remember that the real estate renaissance is not just about buildings and infrastructure—it's about people and communities. It's about creating spaces where people can live, work, and play in harmony with one another and with the natural world. It's about building a future where everyone has the opportunity to thrive, regardless of their background or circumstances.

Thank you for joining us on this journey. May the lessons and insights shared in these pages inspire you to continue your own efforts to revitalize communities and create a better world for future generations. Together, let us continue to write the story of the real estate renaissance—one chapter at a time.

www.ingramcontent.com/pod-product-compliance
Lightning Source LLC
Chambersburg PA
CBHW050237230526
45470CB00005B/2001